The Bible on
Marriage,
Divorce,
& Remarriage

DOUG BATCHELOR

Roseville, CA

Published by
Amazing Facts, Inc.
P. O. Box 1058
Roseville, CA 95678-8058
1 (800) 538-7275
www.AmazingFacts.org

Cover design by Haley Trimmer
Text design by Greg Solie • AltamontGraphics.com

ISBN 978-1-58019-378-8

Table of Contents

Dedication 4

Introduction • A Lasting Knot. 5

1. Happily Ever After 9

2. The Scourge of Divorce 11

3. The Hard Questions. 17

4. Failed Expectations 21

5. Most Sacred Institution 25

6. Conditional Commitment 27

7. Pomp and Circumstance 31

8. One Plus One Equals One. 33

9. Civil Responsibility?. 35

10. Multiple Marriages. 39

11. Adultery. 41

12. Seven Proven Tips for
    Avoiding Adulterous Pitfalls 45

13. Pandemic of Pornography. 47

14. Surviving Adultery. 51

15. Abandonment. 55

16. Separation 59

17. The Blame Game. 63

18. If Divorce Happens. 67

19. Get a New Life. 71

20. Remarriage 75

21. Remarriage and Membership 79

22. Grace for the Fallen 85

23. Tips for a Happy Marriage 91

Dedication

Dedicated to my girlfriend Karen, who also happens to be my wife. She freely sacrificed time that should have been hers so I could wax eloquent about marriage ... what's with that?

And to the memory of my grandparents, Albert and Lillian Tarshis. Married 72 years, in sickness and in health, in prosperity and in adversity, in ketchup and in knitting yarn.

Introduction • **A Lasting Knot**

"Knit your hearts with an unslipping knot."
—*William Shakespeare*

According to the legend, Gordias was a poor Greek peasant who became king of Phrygia under very odd circumstances. He was crowned following a bizarre prophecy spoken by a local oracle, who commanded citizens to select as ruler the first person who rode into the public square in a wagon. Gordias was the lucky man.

In gratitude for his change of fortune, Gordias dedicated his wagon to Zeus and, with a strong, thick rope, tied down the tongue of the wagon securely in the temple grove. The massive, tight knot was so intricately entwined, with the rope ends tucked away inside, that no man's fingers or mind could unravel it. Many tried but failed. However, one day another prophet said that whoever succeeded in loosing the difficult "Gordian Knot" would become the next ruler of all of Asia.

For 100 years the massive knot endured … until a 23-year-old Macedonian ruler invaded Asia Minor and arrived in the city of Gordium. Hearing of this prophecy, the ambitious monarch unsuccessfully attempted to untie the complex knot. Frustrated, the young king stood up, drew his sharp sword, and cut through the rope with a single stroke. Alexander the Great, of course, went on to become the ruler of Asia and beyond.

Today the expression "to cut the Gordian Knot" is commonly used for resolving a difficult problem by a quick and decisive action. Scripture, however, speaks of another solid bond, a knot created by sacred vows before heaven and earth, that is not meant to be so easily severed.

Marriage.

Believe it or not, God never intended marriage to be viewed as a problem to be endured but rather a partnership and blessing to be enjoyed. The Bible declares, "Marriage is honorable," and, "Rejoice with the wife of your youth" (Hebrews 13:4; Proverbs 5:18). Nevertheless, when difficulties arise, many people today quickly reach for the sword of divorce.

Now, perhaps it's a little strange to you that a person named "Batchelor" has written a book about marriage. But be assured, any confusion generated by the pronunciation of my name and the topic of this book is purely coincidental. I am, indeed, a married Batchelor.

With that funny footnote out of the way, this subject is actually a very serious one.

Over the last generation, breakdown of the traditional family and divorce has reached pandemic levels. Even within the Christian church, apathetic attitudes about marriage, divorce, and remarriage are largely just a mirror of those in the world.

But did you know that the fall of virtually every great empire has been preceded by the disintegration of the marriage covenant and the family? Based on history, if this trend is not reversed, the doom of our nation is certain.

As a pastor for 30 years, I have conducted many weddings. Knowing the sobering statistics regarding divorce that newlyweds face, I pray during those sacred occasions for wisdom and wonder if there is anything else I can do or say during the service to help "tie the knot" more securely. I want to tuck away the ends of the rope so that divorce is never even considered as an option.

Ultimately, I realize that true contentment in the home and in a marriage will never be found in the horizontal realm, person to person, until it is first discovered in the vertical relationship between you and God, the maker of marriage.

It is not the purpose of this short book to cover all of the complex variables in the areas of marriage, divorce, and remarriage—there just isn't enough space. Rather, this small work is designed to provide a basic overview and offer essential biblical principles, sprinkled with a few kernels of practical wisdom here and there.

It is also written with a sincere prayer that it might contribute to the healing of struggling marriages everywhere and guide them into stability and true happiness. I pray that the husband and wife of each relationship reading this book might be one and make the honor of God the supreme goal in their lives together.

—Doug Batchelor

Chapter 1 • **Happily Ever After...**

"Don't marry for money; ye'll borrow it cheaper."
—*Scottish Proverb*

Many still remember the wedding of the millennium: Diana Spencer to Prince Charles.

Widely billed as the fairytale story of a beautiful common girl who marries a prince, the royal wedding was broadcast around the world to a television audience of 750 million, while 600,000 people lined the streets just to catch a glimpse of Diana en route to the ceremony.

Diana wore a pricey white dress with a 25-foot train, and the guest list read like a "who's who" of the world's richest and most famous citizens.

It was a wonderful picture of hope and promise ... but a lavish wedding does not a loving marriage make. As we all know, within a decade the "wedding of the millennium" unraveled into just another miserable marriage that ended in sordid stories of infidelity and divorce. What made it even sadder was Diana had herself come from a broken home. Her mother had divorced her father when Diana was very young. On the day Diana's mother left the house, she said to her little girl, "I will be back very soon."

"Very soon" turned out to be never, and that event deeply impacted Diana for the rest of her short life. In fact, after Diana first met Prince Charles (who was actually going out with her sister at the time), she told her friends that she was going to marry him. Her friends wondered how she could possibly know that.

Diana responded, "Because he's the only man on the planet who is not allowed to divorce me."

No human promise, wisdom, or wealth can keep a marriage together; sin has infected our lives too much for that. But the Bible has the keys to make a marriage a happy and productive one—and avoid the scourge of divorce.

Chapter 2 • The Scourge of Divorce

"It is not marriage that fails; it is people that fail."
—Harry Emerson Fosdick

According to statistics gathered by the U.S. Census Bureau, in 1900 the rate of divorce was about 1 in every 100 marriages. By the time the Great Depression rolled around in the 1930s, the divorce rate had climbed to about 5 per 100 marriages. Following World War II, the divorce rate continued to increase to 11 in 100 marriages.

From there divorce rates rose relentlessly, taking a big jump in the 1970s. This might have been due in part to "no-fault divorces" that had become available during that time. Before this, anyone who wanted to end their marriage had to prove their spouse committed adultery or was otherwise relentlessly cruel in their treatment.

And things are only getting worse for marriage. In a 2010 Pew /*TIME* magazine poll, it was revealed that 4 out of every 10 Americans think that marriage is becoming obsolete.

Yet while our culture at large might be growing increasingly ambivalent toward marriage, regarding it as an outdated ancient tradition, God's Word is clear that this institution, created at the beginning of time, is the foundation of a healthy family and nation. Ultimately, marriage is God's idea, which perhaps explains why there is such devastation when a marriage ends in divorce.

The plague of divorce is now so common in our society that it's doubtful there is a soul in America who hasn't been impacted by it one way or another. Perhaps you've been through it yourself … or perhaps a friend, parent, or child of yours.

My mother was married four times; my father, five. I've had stepmothers, stepfathers, and stepsiblings. We've all seen it, and we all know, at least to some degree, the suffering that divorce can bring. This is particularly true for children, who—not understanding what has happened in their home—suddenly find their whole world shattered in ways that leave them picking up the pieces long into their adult years.

The statistics are terrible enough: Between 40 and 50 percent of all first marriages end in divorce. That means almost half the people who get married will, sooner or later, divorce. What's worse is that 67 percent of second marriages will end in divorce too. Perhaps third marriages are charmed? Not at all, as about 74 percent of those go down the tubes as well. Indeed, about 25 percent of adults in America (18 years old and older) are divorced.

Meanwhile, more than one million children each year in America experience the breakup of their parents. *One million!*

What's even more disturbing is that this number *has gone down;* in fact, there are fewer divorces now than there were about 35 years ago. Of course, this probably sounds like good news—but not when you consider the reason. You see, the cause of this decline is simply that the number of marriages has decreased. With the exploding number of unmarried couples living together, the number of recorded marriages and divorces has also declined.

Either way, those are still only numbers … mere statistics.

God knows the very real heartache, the suffering, and the trauma experienced by those who are directly impacted by divorce.

While at the University of California at Berkeley, Dr. Judith Wallerstein led a famous 25-year study on children who came from divorced homes, following them for decades after the divorce. What she found was that, contrary to the popular saying that "children bounce back quickly," they did no such thing. The negative effects of divorce lasted long into adulthood.

In her bestselling book *The Unexpected Legacy of Divorce*, Wallerstein writes about a deeply depressing part of her research, which is the only long-term, close-up study of divorce ever conducted. What she found remains very disturbing. In the introduction, she admits,

> "When I began studying the effects of divorce on children and parents in the early 1970s, I, like everyone else, expected them to rally. But as time progressed, I grew increasingly worried that divorce is a long-term crisis that was affecting the psychological profile

of an entire generation. I caught glimpses of this long-term effect in my research that followed the children into late adolescence and early adulthood, but it's not until now—when the children are fully grown—that I can finally see the whole picture. Divorce is a life-transforming experience. After divorce, childhood is different. Adolescence is different. Adulthood—with the decision to marry or not and have children or not—is different. Whether the final outcome is good or bad, the whole trajectory of an individual's life is profoundly altered by the divorce experience."

Wallerstein also found that:[1]

- Within five years of the divorce, more than a third of the children experienced moderate or severe depression.

- At 10 years, a significant number appeared to be troubled, drifting, and underachieving.

- At 15 years, many struggled to establish strong love relationships of their own in adulthood.

According to another survey, a significant percentage of children from divorced families felt that:[2]

---

1   *Readers Digest*, July 1993, pg. 118ff. Judith Wallerstein and her staff interviewed middle-class children in the San Francisco area.

2   Elizabeth Marquardt, *Readers Digest*, June 2006, pgs. 161–163.

- They were not the center of their family.

- They weren't emotionally safe.

- They couldn't look to their parents for comfort.

- And, while they loved their parents, they didn't necessarily respect them.

Of course, most of us don't need an extensive professional study to know the terrible effect of divorce on children. All one has to have been is a child who has been through his or her parents' divorce. They know how it defines their adult experience.

Just ask one. There are plenty to choose from.

Chapter 3 • Is Divorce Disgrace?

"You can never be happily married to another until you get a divorce from yourself. Successful marriage demands a certain death to self."
—*Jerry McCant*

Russian writer Leo Tolstoy once wrote, "Happy families are all alike; every unhappy family is unhappy in its own way."

In the same way, though there are all sorts of reasons for divorce, each divorce comes with its own unique factors. However, a few things they all have in common are selfishness and pride; each are contrary to what God has always wanted for human beings. God created marriage, not divorce, in the garden of Eden. "For the LORD God of Israel says That He hates divorce, For it covers one's garment with violence" (Malachi 2:16).

Divorce has come into the world only because of sin. It was never meant to be part of the human experience. Jesus Himself all but said as much when the Jewish leaders confronted Him about divorce:

"The Pharisees came and asked Him, 'Is it lawful for a man to divorce his wife?' testing Him. And He answered and said to them, 'What did Moses command you?' They said, 'Moses permitted a man to write a certificate of divorce, and to dismiss her.' And Jesus answered and said to them, 'Because of the

17

hardness of your heart he wrote you this pre-
cept. But from the beginning of the creation,
God "made them male and female." "For
this reason a man shall leave his father and
mother and be joined to his wife, and the two
shall become one flesh"; so then they are no
longer two, but one flesh. Therefore what God
has joined together, let not man separate'"
(Mark 10:2–9).

No question that divorce was never meant to be.

Of course, neither were evil, sin, sickness, suffering, and death. This doesn't mean that all divorce is
sin; it means only that all divorce—as with sickness,
suffering, and death—is the fallout of sin.

Though God never intended for humans to divorce, He has tolerated it under certain conditions.
The questions that believers have long struggled with,
and still do, have to deal with what these conditions
are and what happens if someone violates them.

These are still hotly contested and debated today,
especially in a world in which biblical values are fast
eroding. Frankly, it's just sad and embarrassing that divorce is a major problem in the church. It is a scourge
to which no one is immune. Yet those who care about
doing the right thing, even in a bad situation, can look
to the Word of God for guidance.

Even with the stigma of divorce within the church
and community, there is grace. We must realize that
we all are sinful and are in need of divine mercy. The
point of this book is not to judge others; the point is

to help people know God's will for their lives and to bring healing, grace, and comfort to those who have been traumatized by the possibility or the experience of divorce.

Chapter 4 • Failed Expectations

*"Marriage is an alliance entered into by a man
who can't sleep with the window shut, and a
woman who can't sleep with the window open."*
—*George Bernard Shaw*

I remember hearing years ago that the Hayden Planetarium, which was just across the street from where I grew up in New York City, issued an invitation to anyone interested in being considered as part of the crew on the first journey to another planet. Eighteen thousand people applied. The applications were submitted to a panel of psychologists, who examined each one. Before long they came to the conclusion that the vast majority of those who applied did so because they were disappointed with their lives on earth and hoped they could find a better life somewhere else.

Alexander Pope said, "Blessed is he who expects nothing, for he shall never be disappointed." But we all know that people generally enter the marriage experience with great, but often unrealistic, expectations. This invariably leads to corresponding disappointments.

In Chuck Swindoll's book *The Great Awakening*, he reveals the results of a survey of thousands of men and women about their primary needs in a marriage:

The five major needs women expressed were:

1. Affection
2. Conversation

3. Honesty/Openness

4. Financial support

5. Family commitment

The five major needs men expressed were:

1. Sexual fulfillment

2. Recreational companionship

3. An attractive spouse

4. Domestic support

5. Admiration/Respect

It doesn't take long to deduce that, with such broadly different needs and expectations, this sets up a perfect formula in which someone is going to be disappointed.

In fact, it's safe to say that all divorces have some things in common: failed expectations.

As already stated, each divorce comes with its own unique set of circumstances; however, they also stem from some fairly common reasons. Here are 20 of the most cited:

1. Poor or lack of communication

2. Lack of commitment to the marriage

3. Financial problems/Spend and saving habits

4. Dramatic changes in priorities (both personal and career)

5. Failed expectations or unmet needs

6. Addiction to alcohol and/or some substance

7. Lack of conflict resolution skills

8. Infidelity/Adultery

9. Physical, sexual, or emotional abuse

10. Abandonment

11. Major personality conflicts or "irreconcilable differences"

12. Different expectations about having or rearing children

13. Interference from parents, siblings, or in-laws

14. Intellectual and sexual incompatibility

15. Traditions and cultural lifestyle differences

16. Personal immaturity and "falling out of love"

17. Religious conversion or religious beliefs

18. Inability to deal with each other's idiosyncrasies

19. Mental illness or instability

20. Criminal behavior/Incarceration for crime

If it's any encouragement, many dedicated couples could certainly identify with several of these causes and are still in committed and, yes, even happy marriages. Of course, many other things could be added to the list, but the point is that marriages face multiple strains. Unless two people are deeply committed to making the marriage work, that marriage is in trouble and will always be on the verge of collapse.

Remember also that married life is not a sprint; it's a marathon.

It's also like running a farm. You have to start over every single day. Storms and crop failures in a marriage don't always lead to divorce, but as the numbers show, they often do, and the consequences are always painful.

Chapter 5 • **Most Sacred Institution**

"Chains do not hold a marriage together. It is threads, hundreds of tiny threads, which sew people together through the years."
—Simone Signoret

On January 3, 2004, pop star Britney Spears shocked her fans when she impulsively married her childhood friend Jason Alexander in Las Vegas.

Within 55 hours the marriage was annulled.

Spears said, "I do believe in the sanctity of marriage; I totally do." But she confessed, "I was in Vegas, and it took over me, and, you know, things got out of hand."

One obvious reason many people so recklessly jump into marriage is that they figure if it doesn't work out they can just as quickly jump out. The solemn vows, they reason, are just a required formality.

However, the Bible is not silent regarding the sanctity of marriage. How could it be silent when marriage was created by God? We should expect that the Bible would come with some strict guidelines about what is permitted to cancel a marriage. The many civil and religious laws established to preserve marriage exist because of the high priority of the institution. After all, how important would marriage be if it could be so easily dissolved? If you could be released from this solemn covenant for the most trivial of reasons, then marriage itself would be trivial—and, as we've noted already, this is exactly what's happening in our culture because marriage is so easy to escape.

Salvation is also a sacred covenant. We might have cause to worry if God honored His covenant to save us the same way many people these days honor their marriage vows.

Fort Knox is one of the most heavily guarded locations in North America. Why? Because its vaults contain approximately 4,600 tons of gold bullion. However, grocery stores are not built like small fortresses—with thick walls, armed guards, and complicated safes—to protect bubblegum. The value of what is inside a location is often best revealed by the level of security protecting it.

It's the same with marriage. God has placed a formidable wall, a holy hedge, around this institution in order to protect it precisely because it is so valuable, so sacred, so important. The marriage vow is not like children on a playground making fanciful pledges like, "Cross your heart and hope to die." When a man and woman get married, they are committing themselves to each other in the strongest possible terms. It is a solemn oath made in the presence of God, meant to last as long as those two hearts keep beating in stereo.

"For You have blessed it, O LORD, and it shall be blessed forever." —1 Chronicles 17:27

Chapter 6 • **Conditional Commitment**

*"Success in marriage does not come
merely through finding the right mate,
but through being the right mate."*
—*Barnett R. Brickner*

Joseph Campbell said, "Marriage is not a love affair. A love affair is a totally different thing. A marriage is a commitment to that which you are. That person is literally your other half. And you and the other are one. A love affair isn't that. That is a relationship of pleasure, and when it gets to be unpleasurable, it's off. But a marriage is a life commitment, and a life commitment means the prime concern of your life. If marriage is not the prime concern, you are not married."

But what if you are thoroughly convinced that you married the wrong person? Does the vow still need to be kept … *really?* Psalm 15:1 says, "Lord, who may abide in Your tabernacle? Who may dwell in Your holy hill?" In other words, who will go to heaven? Part of the answer is found in verse 4: "He who swears to his own hurt and does not change." It's talking about a person who has made a promise he doesn't really want to keep anymore, but he keeps it anyway because it was a promise.

It's someone like Jephthah, who promised to dedicate to the Lord whatever came out of his gates when he returned home victorious. (See Judges 11:30.) He likely thought it would be a goat or a cow, but it turned out to be his daughter. Who could have blamed him for taking back that pledge? Yet with a broken heart,

27

he kept his vow, and she was given to serve in the temple for the rest of her life without marrying.

When you stood at the altar and made your vow, did you not know that someday your husband or wife might have days when they act grumpy and look frumpy? Did you never consider that their outward beauty and rippling muscles would eventually sag? They might even snore or someday grow senile and need your constant care. There is no excuse abandoning your sacred vow because it hurts you.

Remember, the kind of love spoken of in the Bible is an unconditional love. "The LORD has appeared of old to me, saying: 'Yes, I have loved you with an everlasting love; Therefore with lovingkindness I have drawn you'" (Jeremiah 31:3). This is the way Jesus loves us. It's not because we are always lovable, but because He has chosen to love us despite our failures. It's not a love driven because of what you do for Him. "For I am persuaded that neither death nor life, nor angels nor principalities nor powers, nor things present nor things to come, nor height nor depth, nor any other created thing, shall be able to separate us from the love of God which is in Christ Jesus our Lord" (Romans 8:38, 39).

It's a choice to love regardless of whether or not a spouse is always lovable.

Inseparable love? *That's* commitment.

Martin Luther said, "The Christian is supposed to love his neighbor, and since his wife is his nearest neighbor, she should be his deepest love."

It reminds me of the poem that I wrote to Karen, my wife, when we got married:

My Promise

As we embark together on this path of life,
You're facing great uncertainties when you
become my wife.
It may be feast, it may be famine, days of
gloom or spirit soaring,
But one thing I promise dear, it never will
be boring.

Today I pledge my love to you and that will
never change,
But health or wealth or circumstance the
Lord may rearrange,
Sometimes in raging waters, sometimes with
battle roaring,
But one thing I promise dear, it never will
be boring.

A castle on a mountain, I cannot guarantee,
Or the time of life we live is not revealed to
me.
But you will always find me at your side
adoring,
And, of course, I promise dear, it never will
be boring.

(So far, I've kept my promise.)

Chapter 7 • Pomp and Circumstance

"A wedding anniversary is the celebration of
love, trust, partnership, tolerance, and tenacity.
The order varies for any given year."
—Paul Sweeney

Despite the recent trend in public opinion polls in America, there is certainly worldwide cultural evidence for the significance of marriage and the importance of the vows as seen in the great occasion made of the event itself.

The wedding of Vanisha Mittal, daughter of the world's eighth richest person, to investment banker Amit Bhatia is arguably the most expensive wedding ever in world history. The six-day event was held in France in 2004, in the Palace of Versailles—the only private function ever held in the palace. The celebration included a reenactment of the couple's courtship and performances by superstars Shah Rukh Khan and Kylie Minogue.

The bill? The father spent $55 million to see his daughter happily linked.

It seems that every year people go to greater lengths to make their weddings more unique and memorable. Not everyone can afford million-dollar weddings, but they certainly strive to mark the occasion with great significance no matter how much money they have.

Indeed, when they don't have the money, they'll try to compensate with the bizarre.

Perhaps you've heard about the New York couple who got married in a shark tank circled by the menacing predators. The bride wore a white wetsuit, and the groom wore a "traditional" black wetsuit. They climbed inside the 120,000-gallon tank to take their vows at Atlantis Marine World in Riverhead, New York. (The one officiating the marriage did so by microphone.)

Then there was a couple in Brussels, Belgium, who took their vows on a bungee jump platform 160 feet in the air. Of course, they took "the plunge" immediately after exchanging their vows. And the list goes on of memorable weddings.

There are only a few really monumental occasions in life—a birth, a death, a graduation, and a marriage. The fact that we make such a big deal about a wedding indicates the considerable importance attached to the covenant. Let's face it: People don't cancel their plans, buy expensive gifts, and fly across the country to witness someone getting their drivers license.

God officiated at the wedding of Adam and Eve, and Jesus' first miracle was at a wedding. The wedding occasion is one of the most important and sacred events in every human culture because two families are being joined. They come together to witness the miracle of a new family being born as one flesh. They come to affirm and support the belief that even in this selfish world, true love can prevail.

Chapter 8 • One Plus One Equals One

"It's easy to understand love at first sight, but how do we explain love after two people have been looking at each other for years?"
—*Unknown*

The deep-sea angler is a very interesting ocean fish. The female is about as big as a volleyball. On the other hand, the male is disproportionately small, like a black jellybean with fins. He has small hook teeth that he uses to bite the female of his dreams and attach himself to her. Once attached, his blood vessels actually join with those of the female—and he will spend the rest of his life merged with her like an extra appendage, getting all of his nourishment from her body in return for fertilizing her eggs. The flesh of the two fish eventually fuses, and they remain permanently connected.

This might not be the most elegant word picture, but it adds new meaning to the Scripture, "Therefore shall a man leave his father and his mother, and shall cleave unto his wife: and they shall be one flesh" (Genesis 2:24 KJV).

Consider the word "cleave" used in this verse; it comes from the Hebrew word *dabaq*, which means "adhere" or "glue." In other words, husbands and wives should be super-glued together in their marriage.

There are several ways that a husband and wife become one flesh. The most obvious is when their chromosomes blend together through an act of love to form a new creature, a child made in their image.

33

However, whether or not they have children, this oneness also applies to the spiritual, mental, and physical aspects of their lives and partnership.

According to researchers at the University of California in San Francisco, when a man and woman engage in sexual intimacy, the hormone **oxytocin** is released, which helps bond the relationship. Oxytocin has been shown to be "associated with the ability to maintain healthy interpersonal relationships and healthy psychological boundaries with other people." When it is released during sex, it begins creating an emotional bond between individuals. Oxytocin is also associated with mother/infant bonding because it is released during childbirth and breastfeeding.

Let's be clear though: When a man and woman get married, becoming "one flesh" is far beyond sexual or chemical. Emotions, dreams, responsibilities, and relationships are all melded together. We have all heard stories of how difficult and dangerous it can be to separate conjoined twins when arteries, nerves, and organs are shared. Likewise, separating what God has joined together seldom happens without great risk. A man and woman in marriage become so closely united in purpose, being, and existence, it is as though they were literally "one flesh." And two lives so intertwined cannot be divided without causing great pain, emotional bleeding, and scarring. That's why divorce is always so devastating.

Chapter 9 • Civil Responsibility?

"The sum which two married people owe to one another defies calculation. It is an infinite debt, which can only be discharged through eternity."
—Johann Wolfgang von Goethe

It has been recognized from ancient times that the strength and health of a nation will mirror the strength and health of its families. As go the marriages of husbands and wives, so go the families and communities, the states and nations. The integrity of the marriage commitment is to a church and country what concrete mortar is to a brick wall.

In 1947, Dr. Carle Zimmerman wrote the book *Family and Civilization*. He studied and tracked the decline of several great empires and discovered eight patterns of domestic behavior that signaled the decline of a civilization. I will only mention the first two precursors, which have to do with marriage and family:

1. The breakdown of marriage and rise of divorce.

2. The loss of the traditional meaning of the marriage ceremony.

When Jesus said, "What God has joined together, let not man separate," He was expressing just how seriously the marriage vow must be taken (Matthew 19:6). In fact, Jesus expressed the sanctity of the wedding vow in the context of divorce. Here is the central statement from Jesus about divorce:

"The Pharisees also came to Him, testing Him, and saying to Him, 'Is it lawful for a man to divorce his wife for just any reason?' And He answered and said to them, 'Have you not read that He who made them at the beginning "made them male and female," and said, "For this reason a man shall leave his father and mother and be joined to his wife, and the two shall become one flesh"? So then, they are no longer two but one flesh. Therefore what God has joined together, let not man separate.' They said to Him, 'Why then did Moses command to give a certificate of divorce, and to put her away?' He said to them, 'Moses, because of the hardness of your hearts, permitted you to divorce your wives, but from the beginning it was not so. And I say to you, whoever divorces his wife, except for sexual immorality, and marries another, commits adultery; and whoever marries her who is divorced commits adultery'" (Matthew 19:3–9).

If this were the only statement in the Bible regarding marriage, it would seem that according to Jesus, there isn't really even one biblical ground for divorcing and then remarrying. Of course, the Bible and Jesus have more to say on marriage than just this passage.

Yet however strict this passage might appear to be, it's simply used here to show, again, how sacrosanct marriage is supposed to be and why a couple, a church community, and even nations are under a divine obligation to protect it.

Chapter 10 • Multiple Marriages

"He who insists upon having all
will have to give up all."
—*Arabian proverb*

Warren Steed Jeffs was the president of the Fundamentalist Church of Jesus Christ of Latter Day Saints from 2002 to 2007. In 2006 he was placed on the FBI Ten Most Wanted list and arrested a few months later. The government wasn't particularly bothered that Jeffs had somewhere between 40 and 50 wives and approximately 56 children. Their main concern was the age at which some girls were being pressed into marriage—the youngest about 15 years old.

While God hates divorce, there is a time or two in the Bible when He actually commands it. For example, whenever someone got married to a person whom they later discovered was still legally married to another ... or several others ... they were to end the marriage.

For instance, when Abraham had taken one wife too many, God told him to "put away" Hagar, his second wife, or concubine (Genesis 21:9–14). So according to the Bible, the act of polygamy is a biblical ground for divorce.

In the beginning, we see God's ideal plan. He made Adam and Eve—not Adam and Eve and Trixy and Jane. A New Testament writer teaches that a man is fit to be an elder only if he "is blameless [and] the husband of one wife" (Titus 1:6). At its most basic level, this means one wife at a time.

Of course, it is true that God did make some laws in the Old Testament regarding how a second wife should be treated; however, this in no way teaches it was part of His plan. (See Deuteronomy 21:15.) Rather, God saw what men were doing and made laws to protect their concubines from mistreatment.

In the book of Ezra, the godly scribe commanded the Jews to put away their pagan wives who they had recently married after returning to the Promised Land. Chances are that many of these wives were second wives or concubines. "By the first day of the first month they finished questioning all the men who had taken pagan wives. ... And they gave their promise that they would put away their wives; and being guilty, they presented a ram of the flock as their trespass offering" (Ezra 10:17–19).

The Word of God identifies another situation in which divorce is permissible, which we'll cover next.

Chapter 11 • **Adultery**

*"It is as absurd to say that a man can't love one
woman all the time as it is to say that a violinist needs
several violins to play the same piece of music."*
—Honoré de Balzac

Every year in North America, about 80,000 deer
die after being struck by motorists on state high-
ways. The peak season for these road kills is the late
fall. Why? Bucks are typically in rut in November;
they are concentrating so much on reproductive ob-
jectives that they are oblivious to other dangers.

Deer aren't the only ones destroyed by a preoc-
cupation with sex.

The Bible says, "Drink water from your own
cistern, And running water from your own well"
(Proverbs 5:15). People begin their marriages with the
best of intentions. Sacred vows are exchanged, sincere
promises are made, and the marriage begins with love
and high hopes. Yet according to the *Journal of Couple
and Relationship Therapy* in 2008, approximately 50
percent of married women and 60 percent of married
men will have an extramarital affair at some time in
their marriage. (We can only hope that these statistics
are more promising among Christians.)

These numbers represent a huge jump from the
previous decade. A University of California study
in 1998 reported that only 24 percent of men and
14 percent of women were sexually unfaithful to
their spouses.

So why the big increase in only 10 years? Probably several factors. The proliferation of TV programs that undermine traditional marriage and normalize casual sex have certainly taken their toll. But the biggest culprit in my opinion is the Internet. The explosion of singles, dating, and sex websites has provided a faucet of constant temptation to every home computer.

We always think of adultery as leading to divorce, and it certainly can, but according to Jesus divorce can also lead to adultery: "Furthermore it has been said, 'Whoever divorces his wife, let him give her a certificate of divorce.' But I say to you that whoever divorces his wife for any reason *except sexual immorality* causes her to commit adultery; and whoever marries a woman who is divorced commits adultery" (Matthew 5:31, 32, emphasis added).

Here we see laid out more clearly the biblical grounds for divorce. The Greek word for "sexual immorality" here is "porneia," from which we get the word "pornography." (We'll address pornography more a little later.) Different versions of the Bible translate this word in different ways, such as "marital unfaithfulness" (NIV); "unchasity" (RSV); and "immorality" (NASB). The bottom line is that the Bible is addressing some form of sexual infidelity here, whether it's adultery, homosexuality, incest, or the like. Though trivialized and made so common by fallen humanity, sexual intimacy is as sacred as marriage. When this sacred intimacy is violated, so is the marriage. That's why sexual infidelity is considered such an egregious breach of the marriage covenant.

The most obvious interpretation of "porneia" is adultery, when one partner in the marriage has sexual relations with someone other than his or her spouse—and this includes all forms of sex, such as oral sex. Adultery is a serious sin and a violation of one of the Ten Commandments. In such cases, an offended partner has the biblical right to divorce.

But even in these cases, divorce is not mandatory.

Chapter 12 • Seven Proven Tips for Avoiding Adulterous Pitfalls

"Marriage resembles a pair of [scissors], so joined that they cannot be separated; often moving in opposite directions, yet always punishing anyone who comes between them."
—*Sydney Smith*

Since we're on the topic of marital infidelity, let's not miss the opportunity to discuss some really good tips to spot the onset of such a disaster and prevent adultery from ever invading your marriage.

1. **Don't flirt with anyone other than your spouse.** Flirting is a form of sexual radar to detect interest in another person. If you encounter someone wondering about your availability, talk about your spouse.

2. **Avoid mingling with herds of singles.** Singles are naturally more on the prowl for a partner and are more suggestive and flirtatious in their conversations. Constant association with singles can influence the mindset of a married person.

3. **Don't tell your problems, especially regarding your marriage, to someone of the opposite sex.** This creates intimacy, which can lead to other things. Intimacy occurs when two people spend time together and share each other's problems and secrets.

4. **Married men and women should not have close friends of the opposite sex.** It is one thing to have acquaintances of the opposite sex, but your best friend should be your spouse, not the girl or guy next door, at school, or at work.

5. **Don't allow the opposite sex to visit your home if you are alone.** In like manner, avoid riding alone with the opposite sex in a car, especially at night.

6. **Avoid personal emails or Internet chatting with any member of the opposite sex.** Internet dialogue with the opposite sex should be informational, not intimate.

7. **Do not accept gifts or lunch from someone you think might be attracted to you.** If they want to greet you with a kiss or a hug, extend your hand for a friendly shake.

And remember, maintaining a mindset that infidelity is a deadly plague rather than an intriguing possibility will help you avoid a world of temptation, sin, shame, and heartache.

Chapter 13 • **Pandemic of Pornography**

"I have made a covenant with my eyes; Why
then should I look upon a young woman?"
—Job 31:1

According to Brigham Young University research, there are 68 million search engine requests related to pornography every single day. This would explain why every 39 minutes a new pornographic video is created in the United States and why the pornography industry has larger revenues than Microsoft, Google, Amazon, eBay, Yahoo, Apple, and Netflix combined. Even back in 2006, worldwide pornography revenues ballooned to nearly $100 billion!

Furthermore, 10 percent of adults in America admit to Internet sexual addiction; of that 10 percent, 28 percent are women.

So what about when a wife discovers that her husband is viewing pornography … or vice versa? Is it biblical grounds for divorce?

Pornography is a toxic, sinful, degrading, and addictive practice. Despite how embarrassing you might think it is, if you are trapped in this pit you need to seek out Christian counsel right away. Doing nothing is the most dangerous thing you can do.

However, I don't believe that viewing naked people engaged in sex is the same as the act of adultery and, therefore, does not provide biblical justification for divorce.* One involves thinking it in the heart; the other involves acting it out with a real person.

If a writer pens a novel about murder, he or she will not be arrested for fantasizing about murder. It is not the same thing as making plans to commit murder either. That would be conspiracy, which is a crime. Pornography is essentially fantasizing about adultery. It is true that viewing pornography is generally connected with masturbation, but this does not fit the biblical definition for adultery. There are many levels of this vicarious kind of adultery. It can be reading romance novels, watching soap operas filled with sordid stories of adultery, and all the way to hardcore porn.

In addressing this sensitive subject, I cannot improve on this perceptive comment by Christian author C.S. Lewis:

> "For me the real evil of masturbation would be that it takes an appetite which, in lawful use, leads the individual out of himself to complete (and correct) his own personality in that of another (and finally in children and even grandchildren) and turns it back; sends the man back into the prison of himself, there to keep a harem of imaginary brides. And this harem, once admitted, works against his ever getting out and really uniting with a real woman. For the harem is always accessible, always subservient, calls for no sacrifices or adjustments, and can be endowed with erotic and psychological attractions which no real woman can rival. Among those shadowy brides he is always adored, always the perfect

lover; no demand is made on his unselfishness, no mortification ever imposed on his vanity. In the end, they become merely the medium through which he increasingly adores himself."

Pornography is so destructive to a marriage because, instead of using sex to galvanize the relationship of a husband and wife, a person ensnared by pornography becomes addicted to self-worship and detaches from his or her spouse.

With all this said, fantasizing, however inappropriate—and yes, sinful—for a Christian is still not the same as committing adultery.

Of course, Jesus made it clear that "whoever looks at a woman to lust for her has already committed adultery with her in his heart" (Matthew 5:28). Adultery in the heart, however, doesn't seem to be depicted by Christ as grounds for divorce.

That's why, in the end, going on the assumption that marriage is sacred and should be protected as much as possible, I believe that it's safer to err on the side of a strict interpretation of adultery. If not, then any spouse whose gaze wanders, even once, could be sued for divorce on biblical grounds. In addition, we'd have to ask the question, "How sacred would marriage be if a lustful thought in the heart were enough to dissolve it?"

_____

*If you discover that your spouse is viewing child pornography and you have children, you should quickly seek professional Christian counsel and consider separating until you can confirm the safety of your children.

Chapter 14 • Surviving Adultery

*"It takes two to make a marriage a success
and only one to make it a failure."*
—Herbert Samuel

On Father's Day in 1995, Steve Trotter and Lori Martin went over Niagara Falls together. They actually survived the plunge because they were in a specially designed barrel made from two hot water tanks—each coated with Kevlar—that were welded together; they also had air tanks that could supply oxygen for more than an hour.

I don't recommend going over Niagara Falls for recreation, as many have tried and died. But you still might be surprised how many have survived the plunge.

Infidelity within a marriage is a terribly painful experience. But it can be survived.

Admittedly there is hurt, anger, jealousy, shame, and a whole stew of other emotions. Yet it's vital to remember that although adultery gives the offended spouse the right to divorce, it doesn't mean he or she automatically *has to*. It isn't mandatory, as if adultery *must* lead to divorce. It certainly isn't mandated in the Bible.

In the Old Testament, for instance, the prophet Hosea married a woman who became very unfaithful, and he did all that he could to keep the marriage together despite her infidelities (Hosea 3:1). God also said that the nation of Israel committed adultery many times, yet the Lord frequently forgave her people and took them back (Ezekiel 16:32).

Many marriages damaged by the unfaithfulness of one partner have nonetheless been salvaged. Obviously, there needs to be a spirit of remorse and repentance demonstrated by the guilty party and forgiveness from the one offended. And it takes time to restore trust.

One wise person said, "Many couples would fare much better if they would stop analyzing grounds for divorce and begin seeking grounds for marriage."

However difficult it might be, many couples—especially if children are involved—would do themselves a big favor to try to make the marriage work despite the pain of infidelity. (Remember, second and third marriages have an even lower success rate than first marriages.) This sends a strong message to the children for the rest of their lives of the importance of marriage, forgiveness, reconciliation, and commitment.

It's not easy, and once that trust is broken, the pieces rarely, if ever, are put back together perfectly. The good news is that they don't have to be. It can still work and, in many cases, even better than before. I have heard many couples say following the experience of infidelity, "We are closer now than we ever have been."

Sex, like marriage, is a gift from God; and like marriage, it has been and still continues to be greatly abused. The best course, the only safe course, is for both marriage partners to put a powerful hedge around their home and not allow anyone at all to breach that hedge, especially in the area of sexual intimacy.

Chapter 15 • **Abandonment**

"Let the wife make her husband glad to come home and let him make her sorry to see him leave."
—*Martin Luther*

The Bible addresses another valid reason for divorce: abandonment by an unbelieving partner.

In the secular world, abandonment is generally used as a legal term to describe the failure of a non-custodial parent to provide support to his or her children. But in our context, we are defining abandonment as when a non-believing spouse walks away from a marriage. In some cases, they might even cut off all communication and virtually disappear—leaving the Christian spouse in marital limbo.

> "Now to the married I command, yet not I but the Lord: A wife is not to depart from her husband. But even if she does depart, let her remain unmarried or be reconciled to her husband. And a husband is not to divorce his wife. But to the rest I, not the Lord, say: If any brother has a wife who does not believe, and she is willing to live with him, let him not divorce her. And a woman who has a husband who does not believe, if he is willing to live with her, let her not divorce him. For the unbelieving husband is sanctified by the wife, and the unbelieving wife is sanctified by the husband; otherwise your children

would be unclean, but now they are holy. But if the unbeliever departs, let him depart; a brother or a sister is not under bondage in such cases. But God has called us to peace" (1 Corinthians 7:10–15).

Here Paul deals with the specific case of those who are married to unbelievers—those who aren't Christians. Though the Bible does warn against being unequally yoked with unbelievers (2 Corinthians 6:15), in many cases one person in a marriage becomes a Christian while the other one doesn't.

In these verses, Paul upholds the sacredness of marriage by saying that if you are married to someone who does not believe, yet that person is willing to stay in the marriage, you are obligated to stay in it as well. He's not saying that there might not be other reasons to separate or divorce. He's just saying that one spouse being an unbeliever isn't one of those reasons.

On the other hand, if the unbeliever walks out the door and doesn't want to be part of the marriage any more, the other spouse is free to get a divorce and remarry. They are no longer under any obligation to the marriage.

Having covered that, this is not a decision that should be rushed. Sometimes couples argue and say outlandish things that would be retracted in calmer waters. If your non-Christian spouse throws his or her hands up in the air and announces in a heated moment, "I want out of this marriage. I don't want to be married to a religious fanatic," don't rush out the next day to get an attorney. "By your patience possess your souls" (Luke 21:19).

If you have come to the Lord but the other spouse has not, that person should be your first mission field. An abundance of time should be invested in praying for the conversion of your unbelieving spouse. Moreover, be a good example without badgering them to convert.

> "In the same way, you wives, be submissive to your own husbands so that even if any of them are disobedient to the word, they may be won without a word by the behavior of their wives, as they observe your chaste and respectful behavior" (1 Peter 3:1, 2 NASB).

Only after there is obvious evidence that the marriage is beyond redemption should divorce be reluctantly processed.

In summary, contrasted with the list under the chapter "Failed Expectations," which shows many of the reasons why people get divorced, the Bible lists only two valid reasons in the eyes of God: adultery (including polygamy) and the abandonment of a believer by an unbeliever.

Chapter 16 • Separation

*"One advantage of marriage is that, if
either party falls out of love, it keeps you
together until you fall in again."*
—Judith Viorst

In 1832 Australia established a 69-acre island in Sydney Harbor known as the "Quarantine Station." With the arrival of each ship—carrying goods and settlers from the far-flung corners of the globe—into the busy port came the dreaded prospect of deadly epidemics like smallpox, cholera, influenza, and bubonic plague, which were ravaging the outside world.

To protect the infant nation from a potential pandemic, this quarantine facility was created to act as a protective barrier between it and contagious diseases. It provided time and space for travelers to heal. A cemetery on the island testifies that not everyone recovered.

Sometimes, marriages also need a barrier of separation providing a little time and space to evaluate the future.

Now remember, the very strict biblical rules for divorce show just how sacred God deems our marriage vows. At the same time, however, the question arises, "What about separation?" Many women have found themselves the victims of brutal men who abuse them and/or the children. Husbands find themselves wed to wives who are desperately addicted to alcohol or drugs to the point where it might endanger the children. A woman can even be married to a man who refuses to pay taxes and, because he files taxes jointly, she faces jail time unless she legally separates. Are these spouses supposed to stay in those miserable situations?

Of course not.

Many have rightly separated from their spouses to preserve the safety of themselves and their children. In fact, there are any number of reasons a person can biblically separate from a spouse. Separation, though, is very different from divorce, a distinction that must be kept in mind. "To the married I give charge, not I but the Lord, that the wife should not separate from her husband (but if she does, let her remain single or else be reconciled to her husband)— and that the husband should not divorce his wife" (1 Corinthians 7:10, 11 RSV).

Separation is not the final play; it's just a time out. Some separations might last a weekend, six months, or indefinitely depending on the circumstances.

In some cases, marriages can deteriorate to the point when it is better for a husband and wife to remove themselves from a toxic or dangerous situation. When this happens, the custody of the children, the adjustment of property rights, or even personal protection might make it necessary for a change in marital status, which is sometimes called "legal separation." However, in some civil jurisdictions such a separation can be secured only by divorce.

Let's consider a hypothetical case in point: A Christian couple with three children are doing fine when promising job opportunities prompt them to move to a new community, not far from a casino. The faithful husband and father, who had never gambled before, goes there for lunch one day and is tempted to try the slot machines. (For some, this is all it takes.) He soon graduates to blackjack and the roulette wheel. Before long he is hooked, addicted to gambling as deeply as an addict hooked on meth. Soon he begins lying to his wife and employer about his long lunches and late evenings at the office. He squanders the checking account, then the savings, living a double life and nursing a desperate delusion that he will someday "win it all back."

Eventually his wife discovers the truth. The credit cards are maxed out, and soon bill collectors begin to call. Compounding things, to cope with his guilt he begins to drink—getting drunk often and screaming and threatening the children. She begs him to confront his problem and get help. He makes many promises to reform but nothing changes. Now this working wife and mother is faced with the possibility that she might lose their house and be responsible for all her husband's rapidly mounting debts.

At this point, it certainly is prudent for her to prayerfully consider a legal separation and compel her misguided husband to seek counsel. This must be done with the goal of redeeming the relationship. Remember, "even if she does depart, let her remain unmarried or be reconciled to her husband" (1 Corinthians 7:11).

There are a thousand other scenarios we might consider, but each situation must be viewed on its own terms because each situation is unique. If separation seems necessary, it is strongly recommended this be done with the thoughtful advice of a godly minister and other Christian counselors.

Chapter 17 • The Blame Game

*"Knowing when to say nothing is 50 percent
of tact and 90 percent of marriage."*
—Sydney J. Harris

Immediately following the entrance of sin into
our world, the first married couple—Adam
and Eve—began assigning and deflecting blame
(Genesis 3:12, 13).

Some things never change.

When seeking to better understand biblical
grounds for divorce, we need to address those who
play the game of creating the circumstances for divorce as a way of escaping an unhappy marriage.

For example, a Christian woman might decide
in her heart that she wants out of her marriage but
does not have biblical grounds. So she might close
the door to all marital intimacy, secretly hoping to
drive her husband into the arms of another. Then
she can file for divorce and point the blame at her
husband's infidelity.

Paul addresses this issue:

"Let the husband render to his wife the affection due her, and likewise also the wife to her
husband. The wife does not have authority
over her own body, but the husband does. And
likewise the husband does not have authority
over his own body, but the wife does. Do not
deprive one another except with consent for

a time, that you may give yourselves to fast-
ing and prayer; and come together again so
that Satan does not tempt you because of your
lack of self-control" (1 Corinthians 7:3–5).

Now this verse is not saying that every husband
and wife should always be available to their mate without consideration of their time, health, or feelings. At
the same time, statistics indicate that most divorces
are preceded by a famine of sexual intimacy.

One pastor said, "The problem with many couples
is that they did too much physically before marriage
and not enough after." According to the Scriptures,
sex should never be used as a reward or punishment
device to manipulate your spouse.

Before marriage, every couple wants to believe
that their sex experience within marriage will always
be one of mutual loving, romantic, and passionate
ecstasy sprinkled with terms of endearment. In real-
ity, happy marriages have discovered that there will
be times when sex might be little more than accom-
modating your spouse's need for affection despite how
tired or disinterested you might feel.

Having said that, it is also insensitive and wrong
for a husband or wife to wave an open Bible at their
spouse, point to 1 Corinthians, and say, "I have authority over your body." The point Paul makes is that
they should "come together" on a regular basis so that
Satan does not tempt them to go outside the marriage
for intimacy—not to demand sex.

Back to the blame game: In other cases, a Christian couple might separate over some incompatibilities and then begin to play the waiting game. They wait to see who commits adultery first so the other party can cry "foul," point the finger, and reestablish themselves in the church as the "innocent party." There are many variations of this game, but God sees clearly into every home and heart and will someday expose this terrible hypocrisy.

Chapter 18 • If Divorce Happens

"When marriage becomes a solution
for loneliness, it rarely satisfies."
—Steve Goodier

In a troubled marriage on the verge of divorce, if there are any threads of hope for reconciliation, don't run for a lawyer right away. Sometimes well-meaning friends, especially those who have experienced volatile divorces, will share horror stories and spook you to jump the gun. Many marriages that might have recovered receive the kiss of death because one partner prematurely fires the first shot and gets a lawyer involved. From that point, fear and greed begin to drive the couple further apart.

As an alternative to engaging expensive divorce lawyers, look for a neutral Christian or other objective counselor to provide friendlier mediation. "A soft answer turns away wrath, But a harsh word stirs up anger" (Proverbs 15:1).

Remember, assuming your estranged spouse has not fled the country or been placed in prison for twenty years, and especially if there are children involved, you will still need to interact with this person for the rest of your life—at graduations, birthdays, weddings, etc.—so don't make a bitter enemy of the person you once vowed to love. Your kids will sense the toxic feelings between their divorced parents, and it will only deepen their sorrow and further harm their emotional well-being.

This probably goes without saying, but people who have experienced a bitter divorce don't always think about the fallout of their words. *Never* say disparaging things about your ex-spouse in front of the children. Jesus referred to the commandments when He said, "Honor your father and your mother," and, "He who curses father or mother, let him be put to death" (Matthew 15:4). This tip could actually serve to lengthen the lifespan of your children! "'Honor your father and mother,' which is the first commandment with promise: 'that it may be well with you and you may live long on the earth'" (Ephesians 6:2, 3). If you want your children to respect you, never teach them by word or act to dishonor their other parent.

Another dynamic to consider is church, because a church is an extension of the family. A divorce within a church tends to bleed within the congregation. A difficult division between a husband and wife often has the members taking sides. This is especially true of smaller churches. Whether it's conscious or unconscious, a divorcing couple can sometimes implement "scorched earth" behavior. It does not further the mission of Jesus for an estranged couple to rehearse or rehash their bitter battles among the body of believers. This will exacerbate division, interfere with future reconciliation, and bring reproach on the cause of Christ.

When Joseph discovered Mary was pregnant, before an angel explained the true circumstances, he resolved to protect her reputation and break off their engagement privately. "Then Joseph her husband, being a just man, and not wanting to make her a public example, was minded to put her away secretly" (Matthew 1:19). This is a rule of thumb we should all follow even after a marriage has fallen apart.

Chapter 19 • Get a New Life

*"The gift of singleness is more a vocation than
an empowerment, although to be sure God
is faithful in supporting those He calls."*
—John Stott

Okay. You have experienced a divorce.

This is a traumatic event. It hurts. Plus, the longer you were married, the more difficult divorce can be. All the hopes and dreams you imagined for your future have been devastated. Everything has changed—your identity as a husband or wife or family. You might even battle with a sense of failure and depression. It could mean a change of careers, double expenses, or your first vocation outside the home.

Divorce often represents a lot of frightening changes. But this can also mean a new beginning and tremendous opportunity. There needs to be some time for grieving, but don't drown in the morass of self pity. "Therefore strengthen the hands which hang down, and the feeble knees, and make straight paths for your feet, so that what is lame may not be dislocated, but rather be healed" (Hebrews 12:12, 13).

In fact, being single represents a great opportunity to serve the Lord without distractions:

"But I want you to be without care. He who is unmarried cares for the things of the Lord—how he may please the Lord. But he who is married cares about the things of the world—how he may please his wife. There is a difference between a wife and a virgin. The unmarried woman cares about the things of the Lord, that she may be holy both in body and in spirit. But she who is married cares about the things of the world—how she may please her husband" (1 Corinthians 7:32–34).

Here are a few practical tips to speed your way to the new you:

1. **Rededicate your life to God.** Be determined to obey Him, whatever His will for your life, and He will guide you. "In all your ways acknowledge Him, And He shall direct your paths" (Proverbs 3:6). "Commit your way to the LORD, Trust also in Him, And He shall bring it to pass" (Psalm 37:5).

2. **Trust God to provide.** A divorce is often followed by harsh financial challenges. If you make God, His kingdom, and righteousness first in your life, He promises to provide for your essential needs (Matthew 6:33).

3. **Schedule daily devotions.** Read good Christian inspirational books and avoid television. There are so many references to divorce, adultery, and materialism on TV. And let's face it: Television is designed to make you unsatisfied so you will try to solve your problems by running out and purchasing a product. Instead, plan and schedule to have regular

devotions every day. Time in the Word and in prayer will provide the best foundation for your new life.

4. **Avoid negative people and music.** Steer clear from downer people who love to rehearse the sad past—and avoid listening to sad or melancholy music. "But one thing I do, forgetting those things which are behind and reaching forward to those things which are ahead" (Philippians 3:13).

5. **Take care of your body.** Divorce and depression can lead to overeating and indolence. Weight gain and lack of exercise can also lead to deeper depression. Get out of that vortex immediately. Join a health club. Exercise or walk with positive friends. "He who walks with wise men will be wise" (Proverbs 13:20).

6. **Embrace new challenges in your work.** Whether your work is in the home or office, move the furniture or take on a new assignment or department … or a new job altogether. Volunteer at church. New you, new work.

Chapter 20 • **Remarriage**

*"Loneliness is the first thing that
God's eye named not good."*
—*Milton*

In 1960, 88 percent of men aged 35 to 44 were married; for women it was 87 percent. By 2007 this percentage had fallen to 69 percent for men and 72 percent for women. But if online dating services are any indicator, this trend will change.

The online dating industry is now worth $4 billion worldwide. Amazingly, 17 percent of the couples married in 2009 had started out the relationship on a website. And according to research group Ground Truth, the average user of a mobile phone now spends 12 minutes and 44 seconds on mobile dating sites per week, while mobile dating in general saw a 92 percent increase in users in the summer of 2010.

No question: There are a lot of lonely people out there trying to find someone.

As we've discussed, people choose to divorce for numerous reasons. Sometimes those reasons are biblical; often they are not. What's done is done, and most divorcees eventually get lonely again and begin to yearn for a mate.

The question naturally arises for the Christian, *What about remarriage?*

This can be very difficult, painful, and sticky. How do we defend the sanctity of marriage while at the same time showing the same grace, mercy, and redemption toward others that we would want for ourselves when we need it? We all have our faults and shortcomings and sins.

But let's be bold. According to the Scripture, if someone commits adultery and divorce ensues, the guilty one is not allowed to re-marry. To do so would be to commit adultery again. (See Matthew 19:8, 9; 1 Corinthians 7:1.) It is absolutely appropriate for a church to censure someone who takes this path. But censure is not the same thing as shunning. Everyone should be encouraged to come to church where the Word is proclaimed and conversions and healing often happen. (We'll talk more about this particular challenge for our churches in the next chapter.)

The non-guilty party, of course, is free to remarry if he or she chooses. If this is your case, don't rush. In the event that divorce is unavoidable, loneliness can be compounded by a sense of failure. This is a time when people are especially vulnerable to temptation and jumping prematurely into another serious relationship. Dating or singles websites can accelerate this hasty choice. This is one of the reasons that second marriages are more prone to failure than first marriages. It takes at least a year to rediscover who you are as a single person.

Once again, this is especially true if there are children involved—they could still be going through the grieving process only to suddenly discover that one of their divorced parents is already dating a virtual stranger.

The Bible takes our marriage vows seriously. We ought to as well. The Bible also takes grace for sinners very seriously. We ought to as well. And that includes grace for those who have failed in the area of marriage and remarriage, a failure that is all too common today.

Regardless of how scrambled your nuptial history might be, the promise of Jesus is, "All that the Father gives Me will come to Me, and the one who comes to Me I will by no means cast out" (John 6:37). Jesus also said, "Those who are well have no need of a physician, but those who are sick. I have not come to call the righteous, but sinners, to repentance" (Luke 5:31, 32).

Chapter 21 • Remarriage and Membership

*"If you don't stand for something
you'll fall for anything."*
—Unknown

In 2000, James Dale sued the Boy Scouts of America for expelling him from the organization after discovering his openly homosexual preference and gay rights activism. After years of litigation, the Supreme Court supported the rights of the Scouts, specifically the freedom of association, which allows a private organization to exclude a person from membership when "the presence of that person affects in a significant way the group's ability to advocate public or private viewpoints." The court ruled that opposition to homosexuality is part of the Scouts "expressive message" and allowing homosexuals as leaders would interfere with that message.

The Christian church also has an "expressive message," and membership has its guidelines. We all know that in this world, people get married and divorced willy-nilly and with little social reproof. But the Bible declares there are criteria and consequences for divorce and remarriage that must be addressed by His church.

Several years back, a man stormed uninvited into my office at church. He barked, "I thought you folks were supposed to be Christians? I guess you don't believe in the Ten Commandments anymore!" When I assured him I was listening, he calmed down and related through his heated tears that one of our deacons was having an affair with his wife.

I was sickened when the scandalous charge proved to be true. I was ashamed that one of our members, a leader no less, was parading around that kind of witness in the community. I was especially grieved about what it said about Christ, not to mention our church. Of course, we needed to remove that individual from office and membership.

Because divorce is so prevalent in our society, many churches are reluctant to deal with these very sticky issues and apply biblical discipline. Unfortunately, by their neglect or lack of courage, the plague spreads and the name of Jesus is besmirched.

The apostle Paul addressed a similar issue with the Corinthian believers. Evidently, a young man was sleeping with his stepmother and nobody in the church wanted to deal with this embarrassing situation. "It is actually reported that there is sexual immorality among you, and such sexual immorality as is not even named among the Gentiles—that a man has his father's wife! And you are puffed up, and have not rather mourned, that he who has done this deed might be taken away from among you" (1 Corinthians 5:1, 2).

So what happens when the guilty party in a divorce does remarry, as is so often the case? In such situations, each church must be responsible to deal with the issue in a biblical way. This generally means the name of the offending party should be removed from church membership. Neglecting this somber duty can contribute to spiritual anemia within the congregation. It sends a cancerous message to the next generation that marriage is a trivial institution. "They sow the wind, And reap the whirlwind" (Hosea 8:7).

Many denominations have a marriage and divorce committee to advise and make recommendations in these complex situations. This can help keep the local congregation in a more redemptive relationship with the offender.

Oftentimes, people who divorce without biblical grounds are removed from office and are dropped from the church books. This should always be performed in a graceful way to keep the path for their return clear. If they continue to attend, they might even eventually be allowed back onto the church books after demonstrating repentance and conversion. This should be followed by varying periods of probation. Others might be allowed to stay on the church rolls, though they aren't permitted to hold any kind of church office.

Now this does not mean that those who get divorced and remarried without biblical grounds can say a quick prayer, shed a tear, and then move on within the church as though nothing happened. In the Bible, a person guilty of unintentional manslaughter could flee to a city of refuge and find sanctuary, but they could not go home until the death of the high priest (Numbers 35:28). This often involved years of waiting to be restored, and it might be the same for the marriage transgressor.

As with the case of the following couple, some are good Christians who are just very lonely. They had met online and quickly married. Within a month, they realized it was a disaster of a decision and had the marriage annulled.

They knew they did not have biblical grounds for divorce and recognized it was a terrible mistake … a sin. They were remorseful for their impulsive bad judgment. After carefully considering the issues, the church decided to put them on censure but did not drop their names.

While each case like this must be looked at on its own merits, there should always be some action of discipline or censure. "Those who are sinning rebuke in the presence of all, that the rest also may fear" (1 Timothy 5:20).

It must be kept in mind, though, that a spouse who has violated the marriage vow and led the marriage into divorce does not have the moral right to marry someone else while their first spouse, who has been faithful to the vow, still lives and remains unmarried and chaste. For the guilty one, under those circumstances, to marry again would be compounding their sin.

However harsh that sounds, there's good reason for it. Again, it makes people realize just how sacred the marriage vow really is. Today, with the act of legally divorcing nearly as easy as canceling a credit card, people need to understand the serious nature of marriage and divorce in the eyes of God. How sacred would marriage be if people divorced with impunity for whatever trivial reasons they had and remarried just as quickly, with no questions asked by the church—all as if nothing were wrong? Unfortunately, this is increasingly the norm.

Marriage is supposed to provide a secure place for the whole family. To divorce and remarry outside the strict bounds that God has placed on marriage would remove the protection and safety that marriage brings. Because of this, the church must take the biblical stand on marriage and divorce seriously and deal accordingly with members who violate those positions.

Of course, there are so many other complicated issues in the question of divorce and remarriage, many more than can be covered in this small book. Nevertheless, the point needs to be stressed again and again: Marriage is a sacred covenant to be deeply respected.

Once again, look at the incredible damage that has been done to millions of people because of unfaithfulness in marriage, especially children. The most common fear for children, especially the youngest, is sudden abandonment. For most of them, divorce does not come as a relief to their unhappiness, even when they have been living in a high-conflict family. The home is so special that, no matter how miserable, most children prefer it to having it broken apart. *That says a lot.*

The question is: Are the adults listening?

Chapter 22 • **Grace for the Fallen**

"He who demands mercy and shows none burns the
bridges over which he himself must later pass."
—Thomas Adams

According to a Gallup Poll, "Amazing Grace" is
Americans' favorite hymn. It was written by the
former captain of a slave ship—an atheist, womanizer,
and foul-mouthed drunk. However, that "wretch,"
John Newton, eventually found Christ and experienced grace. He went on to become an Anglican minister and worked to abolish the slave trade.

While it is clear that the Bible demands, with
good reason, that we regard our marriage vows with
the highest level of respect, it also places a great deal
of emphasis on mercy and grace. It teaches that we all
are sinners and that all have fallen short of God's perfect ideal; that includes in our marriages. Who doesn't
know someone in that category? It might be you.

Thus, we need to show patient sympathy, com-
passion, and grace for those who have found themselves in tough marriage situations. Again, each case
must be looked at individually, yet we must adhere to
biblical standards in the context of grace for the fallen.

So, what if someone has been divorced and remarried without biblical grounds? Perhaps their relationship was formed through the adulterous affair
itself. Will God ever accept them as truly married?
Can they ever find peace with God, or is this the
unpardonable sin?

85

Look for a moment at the infamous story of King David and Bathsheba. When Nathan the prophet confronted David regarding his adulterous relationship with Bathsheba, the king freely confessed and sincerely repented of his sin. Still, there were profound consequences:

> "David said to Nathan, 'I have sinned against the LORD.' And Nathan said to David, 'The LORD also has put away your sin; you shall not die. However, because by this deed you have given great occasion to the enemies of the LORD to blaspheme, the child also who is born to you shall surely die'" (2 Samuel 12:13, 14).

The illegitimate baby became deathly sick, so David spent seven days on his face praying for the child and repenting of his sin. Still, the child died. (I frequently meet professed Christians who want forgiveness for a sin like David's but aren't willing to repent like David.)

From this point on God demonstrated His forgiveness for David and accepted that Bathsheba was now his wife. Strong evidence for this is in the fact that the next child Bathsheba bore with David was Solomon, who was chosen by God to be king after David and even an ancestor of Jesus.

> "Then David comforted Bathsheba his wife, and went in to her and lay with her. So she

bore a son, and he called his name Solomon. Now the LORD loved him" (2 Samuel 12:24).

The couple that began their relationship with an adulterous marriage was eventually recognized by the Lord as married. But the consequences of David's sin followed him for the rest of his life.

Then there is the example of the Samaritan woman at the well:

> "Jesus said to her, 'Go, call your husband, and come here.' The woman answered and said, 'I have no husband.' Jesus said to her, 'You have well said, "I have no husband," for you have had five husbands, and the one whom you now have is not your husband; in that you spoke truly'" (John 4:16–18).

No doubt she was stunned that Jesus knew about her ensemble of husbands, even their exact number. She later confessed to her neighbors that Jesus knew "all things that I ever did" (v. 28).

Now Jesus never condemned her, but He let her know that her sins were not hidden from Him. The woman was convicted and went back to witness to her own people. If there were no hope of her being saved, the Lord probably would not have bothered revealing to her that He was the Messiah.

In other words, Jesus knew of her sins and was seeking to save her from them. Again, though we're not told, we can be fairly sure that whenever she got back to her live-in boyfriend, she either married him or kicked him out and ended the relationship. She surely didn't just go back to her old way of life!

The point is that we cannot unscramble scrambled eggs, and while the consequences of our decisions might not ever disappear, God meets us where we are.

Indeed, we also have the touching example of the woman caught in the very act of adultery, described in John chapter 8. After throwing the guilty woman at Jesus' feet, the scribes and Pharisees, implying she should be stoned, began pressing Jesus for a verdict. Christ responded with the immortal words, "He who is without sin among you, let him throw a stone at her first" (John 8:7).

Convicted by their own consciences, the religious leaders withdrew.

Jesus addressed His next comments to the guilty. "'Woman, where are those accusers of yours? Has no one condemned you?' She said, 'No one, Lord.' And Jesus said to her, 'Neither do I condemn you; go and sin no more'" (John 8:10, 11).

Jesus was not excusing adultery; in fact, He clearly identified it as a sin. But that's the important point. Grace and mercy thrive where forgiveness is not deserved.

We must let people know that they can come to the Lord as they are, sinners in need of grace. Divorce without biblical grounds is a sin, but the Bible does not say it is the unpardonable sin. And lest anyone misunderstand, church discipline properly performed is a loving act. But it does not need to be the final act.

The Lord gives us the option to extend to the guilty mercy and re-admittance to the church family when we are led by the Spirit to believe it is the most redemptive course for everyone involved.

Chapter 22 • **Tips for a Happy Marriage**

"Marriage should be a duet; when
one sings, the other claps."
—Joe Murray

Decades ago, American author William Faulkner, commenting about fellow author Ernest Hemingway's third divorce, wrote the following:

> "Poor bloke, to have to marry three times to find out that marriage is a failure, and the only way to get any peace out of it is (if you are fool enough to marry at all) [to] keep the first one and stay as far away from her as much as you can, with the hope of some day outliving her."

What a cynical and sad concept of matrimony!

No question: Marriage can be challenging. But it is *intended* to be a wonderful gift from God—a blessing, not a burden. "He who finds a wife finds a good thing, And obtains favor from the LORD" (Proverbs 18:22).

The key, of course, is communication.

There is a story about an old man and his wife who were celebrating their golden wedding anniversary—50 years of married life. Having spent most of the day with relatives and friends at a big party given in their honor, they returned home. They decided, before retiring, to have a little tea with bread and jam. Seated in the kitchen, the husband opened up a new loaf of bread and handed the end piece (the heel) to his wife. After a long pause, she exploded, saying, "For 50 years you have been dumping the heel of the bread on me. I've held my peace, but enough is enough. I refuse to take it anymore, this lack of concern for me and what I like." On and on she went scolding him. The husband was absolutely astonished at the tirade. When she had finished, another long pause drifted between them. Finally, with misty eyes, he softly said to her, "The heel is my favorite piece."

I say again: Communicate!

Every marriage faces challenges, some big and some small. Life is precious and short; therefore, focus on the larger battles, working through them as a team while letting go of the incidentals that, in the big scheme of things, don't really matter. Choose your battles wisely. If you are going to pick something apart, make sure it's worth the effort. Unfortunately, unresolved arguments are a big issue in marriages, often leading to divorce. Therefore, unless the issue is something significant, learn to let some things roll off your back. When you do discuss the big stuff, wait until you're alone. If the children feel like they're in the bleachers of a boxing match between mom and dad, it can be very troubling.

Below are a few more points that can help make marriage the blessing it was intended to be. Some of these tips might sound like fortune cookie clichés, but they are true nonetheless.

First, one of the most crucial aspects of marriage is practicing forgiveness. Ben Franklin said, "Keep your eyes wide open before marriage, and half shut afterwards." We need to learn to apologize when we are wrong—and if we're smart, we might find something to apologize for even when we know we are right.

As we have been forgiven by God, we should also forgive our spouses, even when they don't deserve it. "Marriage," someone said, "is three parts love and seven parts forgiveness." That's what biblical forgiveness is all about: forgiving the undeserving. If we don't learn to forgive, marriage, if it survives, will be like purgatory.

But you might be asking, "How can I love and forgive a person when they have hurt me so deeply? After I have seen their dark and ugly side. How can I love them when they demonstrate so little love for me?" As you think about these questions, keep in mind these are the very questions Jesus can ask about each of us. Despite our selfishness and sin, He loves and forgives us. He gave His life to be one with us. "Husbands, love your wives, just as Christ also loved the church and gave Himself for her" (Ephesians 5:25).

Second, just as the Bible teaches that we are sinners, we must accept the fact that we are married to someone who is physically, emotionally, and spiritually damaged by sin. Get over it. Your spouse has faults. Marriage is the art of two incompatible people learning to live compatibly. Pray your way through his or her faults. You might have to live with those faults, but you don't have to obsess over them. If you do obsess over them, they will eventually eat you and your marriage alive. A perfect, holy God, through Christ, accepts us as we are; you, who are hardly holy and perfect, must do the same for your spouse. God then transforms us by love. If you would see change in your spouse, exemplify His life and love in your life.

> "So husbands ought to love their own wives as their own bodies; he who loves his wife loves himself" (Ephesians 5:28).

Next, don't always think of yourself first. As fallen humans, our default mode is "Me, Me, Me." Like a compass that always points inward, our first impulse in any situation is to think of ourselves and of our own needs, survival, and comfort before anyone else's— and that, unfortunately, includes our spouses. Try, through God's grace and Spirit, to put your spouse before yourself just as Christ put us before Himself. Such an attitude can, and indeed will, do wonders for any marriage.

And just as Christ put Himself in our situation, for He "was in all points tempted as we are, yet without sin," try to put yourself in your spouse's shoes (Hebrews 4:15). In other words, when a tense situation arises, step back for a few moments and try to see things from your partner's perspective. How does this situation impact him? Why would she feel as she